AT A TANGENT

PREVIOUS BOOKS BY JOHN WESTON

Poetry
Mindful, Shoestring Press, 2023
Echo Soundings, Shoestring Press, 2012
Chasing the Hoopoe, Peterloo Poets, 2005
Take Five 04, Shoestring Press, 2004

AT A TANGENT

New and Selected

JOHN WESTON

All rights reserved. No part of this work covered by the copyright herein may be reproduced or used in any means – graphic, electronic, or mechanical, including copying, recording, taping, or information storage and retrieval systems – without written permission of the publisher.

Printed by imprintdigital
Upton Pyne, Exeter
www.digital.imprint.co.uk

Typesetting and cover design by The Book Typesetters
hello@thebooktypesetters.com
07422 598 168
www.thebooktypesetters.com

Published by Shoestring Press
19 Devonshire Avenue, Beeston, Nottingham, NG9 1BS
(0115) 925 1827
www.shoestringpress.co.uk

First published 2024
© Copyright: John Weston
© Front cover photograph: Gill Marshall-Andrews
© Back cover: Oil painting of author by Peter Edwards

The moral right of the author has been asserted.

ISBN 978-1-915553-57-7

ACKNOWLEDGEMENTS

Among these *New Poems*
now collected for the first time
one or two (or a variation)
did appear earlier,
e.g. in *The Spectator* or in *The Guardian*.

'Balloon over London'
is in the city group of
New Poems, with some
notes about how I conceived
its re-inflation through the breath
of poetry.
I allowed my poem to be printed
in July 4, 2013, as a Found Poem over my name
by the US magazine *Literary Imagination*
in conjunction with Oxford University.

For Sally, my dear wife,
and all our close family.

"Discovering what we see
in the clear half-light
between life at first sight
and its after-glow.

Retreiving what long ago
was forgivably lost
yet at a lasting cost."

— *John Mole*

CONTENTS

Preface   1

from *TAKE FIVE* (2004)

The Launch	5
My Father	6
Scillies in April	7
Last Rites	8
Giving Way	10
Talisman	11
Grandparents	12
First Grandchild	13
Sighting	14
Moving with *The Times*	15
Fifty Years On	17

from *CHASING THE HOOPOE* (2005)

The Slip	23
Taking Down The Cards	24
Image	25
Snow Buntings at Floyd Bennett Field	26
Upwellings	27
A Song of Praise	29
Homage to a Government	31
Still Life in New York	32
The Shillinged Birches	34
Invitation	35
May Lane, Birmingham	36
Elizabeth's Version	37
Peking Rap	39

from *ECHO SOUNDINGS* (2012)

Looking Down MacDougal	45
Kennedy's Latin Primer	46
The Cake Of Custom	48
Turing Test	50
End Game	51
Payload	52
Reception	54
Table Talk	55
Skep	56
Columella's Nipple	57
Reading Aloud	58
Coming Down To Earth	59
Putting The Heart To School	61
Lithium	63
Exercise	64
Serengeti	65
In The Palm House	66

NEW POEMS

Omen	69
Pastoral	70
Alcaics for Brubecks	71
Moments	72
Laying Queen	73
Malus Hupuhensis in April	74
Getting the Bird	75
Birthday Villanelle	76
Sonnet	77
Chinese	78
Slow Light Burning	79
From Short Poems by Shi Tao	80
Trompe l'oeil	81
Villanelle	82
Jigsaw	83
Ham House Party	84
Edwardes Square	85

Pesthouse Common	87
'Lion couchant'	88
One of Those Things	89
Years Go By	90
Goodness Will Out	91
Afterword	92
Golden Jubilee Sestina	93
Ballad of Carragilihy and Inishbofin	95
Wickam	99
A Villanelle from Richard Hakluyt	100
Self Portrait of the NPG	101
A Poem for Kew	102
Olympic Message	103
Balloon Over London	104
Lower West Side 1962	106
Enough and Plenty	107
Uncollected Fragment, 1935	108
In the Loaning	109
Fixed Points	110
Up To Date	111
Teenage Lines	113
Catching Up	114
Retrospective	115
Sonnet for John Burnside	116

PREFACE

In 'Uncollected Fragment, 1935', one of the new poems in this substantial selection from his work, John Weston quotes from the letters of Wallace Stevens: 'Study gives the anchorage / of thought, the place to spring from, and poetry / the adventure'. This in several ways could be seen as reflecting on his own practice as a poet whose attention to detail and relish for what he calls 'the constant surprise of gradualness' is matched by a readiness to take risks and a spirit of adventure. Poems that by turns accumulate and deploy facts and figures that vividly recount experiences abroad and at home, celebrate the natural world's 'whole launch and heave of growing things', mark important occasions, raise contemporary issues, and explore the 'little kindnesses, the hidden complicities' in family relationships all become, for Weston, what poetry is made for and from – those 'pure/singularities, / the flagrant coincidence / that gives you the front seat'. Often witty and self-deprecating, they can also prove to be intimately candid, anchored in thoughts that are sometimes troubled but always imaginatively expressed and resolved. As he writes in 'Coming Down to Earth' 'Grief, like happiness, fulfils itself / shared' and in the moving sequence 'Misfortune Shared', originally published separately in a pamphlet as *Mindful*, charting the illness and recovery of his younger son, he demonstrates this with grace and equilibrium.

Weston enjoys the challenge of received form. 'At a Tangent' contains two accomplished sestinas, the lines of which fall into place without any sense of constraint, sonnets with varying patterns of rhyme, a playful pantoum, a set of alcaics and several villanelles amongst which are one from father to son, alluding to the circumstances that inform 'Misfortune Shared', and a particularly touching 'Birthday Villanelle' for his wife. to whom other poems in the volume are dedicated, including 'Fifty Years On'. Weston is an excellent poet of married love, tender, affectionately reminiscent, detailing various incidents from courtship to becoming grandparents, but never falling into the safety net of mere sentimentality. He also has a strong sense of the dramatic, particularly when recalling incidents from his career as a diplomat in China at the time of the cultural revolution and 'Peking Rap' is delivered with a chilling journalistic brio which makes it one of the highlights of his selection.

In his recent poem remembering John Burnside, a poet he much admires, Weston 'again makes reference to Wallace Stevens, mentioning that the critic Jonathan Bate has compared the two of them as exploring the relationship between the idea and the thing' which also brings to mind William Carlos Williams' asserting 'no idea but in things'. Weston quotes directly from

Burnside who asks 'how to be alive in all this gazed upon / and cherished world, and do no harm' and many of his own poems, vividly and precisely explore aspects of that world, on both a small and large scale, whether gazing upon birds, bees and flowers in the family garden, as in poems such as 'Omen', 'Laying Queen', 'Penthouse Common' and the beautiful little 'Lion Couchant' or, when travelling further afield, exclaiming 'Everywhere such fecundity' in 'Upwellings', a luminous account of travelling in the Galapagos Islands.

John Weston is essentially a celebrant, very much cherishing this world as a witness while at the same time engaging with it, day by day, and accepting its social obligations and invitations. At its core is a strong sense of love and duty, as is evident in the many poems about family and those arising from the demands of his career prior to 2002 when he began writing poetry. A substantial collection in many different modes but always with the same voice, *At a Tangent* consistently returns us, poem by poem, to the centre of what in 'Still Life in New York' its author describes comprehensively as 'a world's circle'.

– John Mole

from *Take Five* (2004)

THE LAUNCH
(For Marcus)

I do not remember the house
where I was born, though the poem
(in my mother's voice) opened on
more than the sun's little window.

I must have grown ears like errant
wings at school when they recited
spells for how the gyre and gimble,
spread butter with the carpenter.

I tasted mellow fruitfulness;
saw silent flock in woolly fold;
wondered about his last duchess,
golden lamps, vegetable love,

and whether fifty springs sufficed
to stop winter icummen in.
I listened to Greek frogs croaking,
the ripple of Sabine fountain.

But you follow jumblies to sea
with 'sails as frail as autumn leaves',
leaving me standing in the lea
with 'less than one good line a day'.

It makes me think of my first bike –
the Coventry, and how they had
to push and push to get me to
take off; and the bird like grace of

equilibrium finally
achieved, the blessing of surprise
at discovering that no hands
could mean flying even faster.

MY FATHER

He emerges from
the pages of his never-
to-be published verse
gesturing to me, as with
some forgotten semaphore –

'The Shrapnel Gleaners',
'Oak Trees', 'Afternoon Alert'.
So I too glean shards
from blitzed childhood memories,
rebuild his fractured presence,

matching his phrases
to precarious glimpses
over a lifetime,
and seeking now to summon
his ghost out of the shadows

for a belated
Festschrift. What coded sequence
has pushed my pen to
themes or images later
found prefigured in his own?

Broken health, broken
love – these poems I value
more now: lineaments
of a disappointed life,
but an honest monument.

It speaks still, the voice
comes and goes, as I read them,
eclipsing absence;
his own words, like a handshake:
"How I pray he will not grieve".

SCILLIES IN APRIL

Running up to the Day-Mark
through spring heather
and high on the evening sea air,
I flushed the distant bird –
it launched on barred wings
sank fast within half a furlong
back into cover.

All the way back at full stretch
I searched my retina's sight-hoard
('look for the field-mark')
to earth the gaudy flash of
harlequin
with a sure connection;
my one recollection surely
too far outlandish.

Only after two days
did I catch Terry's mate on the
'Voyager of St Martin's',
to pep up his passengers, volunteering
"Have you heard, on Chapel Down
they've spotted a
hoopoe?"

O *upupa epops*! O song!
To have been on the mark all along!
Halloo small miracle, strange visitant,
shade of Aristophanes!
Last seen in April seven years ago
on a consular lawn
in Jerusalem.

LAST RITES

That final day in Bedford hospital
the car-park man ticked me off, as I came out
'You can't leave yours there, you know'. 'I do know,'
I answered 'but your mother only dies once'.

She'd never adjusted to life without work –
her bank of interests had too little left to draw on.
So in the small hours, when breathless anxiety struck,
comfort was slight, and I knew I was out of my depth.

'None of that sort of thing in *our* family' she insisted
when I rescued her from a psychiatric ward.
She was convinced they were secretly plotting against her,
which would have been funny except for her haunted eyes.

The end near, I was called to a different bedside.
She seemed more puzzled than frightened, even slightly indignant
when I ventured on her passage from 'Revelation',
as if to say 'Not much of *that* in the family either'.

Her insistent 'Goodbye' at my whispered goodnight
before snatching sleep in an adjacent room
I realised only afterwards had meant what it said,
for with the dawn she sighed deeply, and stopped.

Her face suffused with a Lenten purple blush.
Kneeling I kissed her, drew the rings from her finger,
then rose to leave the orderlies to their business.
I felt she'd launched on Gerontius' great journey,

me on the nearest shore applauding her brave
life and her exit from it. In Ampthill churchyard,
'See, they return, and bring us with them' the stone said.
When at last I went back to clear her belongings,

as if possessed by a sudden mythic force
I fell on her bed, and felt bodying forth
a primal surge, of upwelling torrent of grief
sucking the breath out of me – a raw howl

the ear could hardly recognise as my own.
Knocking at the door, a neighbour below enquired
politely if a cup of tea might help, her gesture
the cue for all the familiars to reassemble.

GIVING WAY
"The Athabasca Glacier has retreated 1.5 kilometers since 1850"

The mountains rose to a spotless sky
that morning as we approached.
At the pass, moonscape:
in a valley bulldozed by behemoth forces,
 acres of claggy moraine and rock.

Walking up over the debris we counted markers
signalling at decade intervals the farthest reach
of the glacier's toe, its secular melt-back.
In a few hundred yards we passed
my birth, my matriculation,
the flurry of children, our retirement.

We ventured onto the ice flow,
the air grew chiller, water chuckled unseen.
Striding ahead up the frozen slope
toward the grin of crevasses
I heard your anxious voice calling me back.

I turned, to recognise I must be standing
on my own graveside, the coming ebb point
where the glacier's, mute recessional
would not mark time for me.

Together again going down, we observed
how alpine fireweed and parnassia
had already begun to repossess the abandoned marl.

As we left the ice field and drove on,
the weather changed.

TALISMAN

This Victorian penny
bullet hole punched at the rim
where it winged the old Queen's crown,
has sat on my key-ring since.

I filched it from *The White Hart's*
till, half a century back,
for luck. FID DEF's never let
me down, though the coin has worn

communion-wafer thin,
and in just one hundred years
the embossed flag has faded
from the shield of Britannia,

whose head (or what was left by
the wound exiting the oth-
er side) is now floating in
the feuillemorte Valhalla cloud.

If I tilt it to the light,
the royal gaze is fixed, but
the lips move, the cheek allows
a faint porphyry blush. Touch,

it's my aged aunt's soft kiss
when she came in from the snow.
I pinch it between my finger
and thumb, chafe the used metal.

GRANDPARENTS

They hover like buddhas over our imaginings,
antique household gods who rode away on clouds
to make room for fresh devotions. Now occasional
visitants, leaning from framed sepia and damask
to enter the seasonal gathering at a happenstance, a phrase.

Down to earth in their day: the old man trying to salvage
a legacy's barren stake in Canadian uplands;
the grand dame, who mothered a tribe of seven
among them my father, making do in the blitzed city
and never revealing her answer to the infant's parroted question
("Granny, do *you* wear fully-fashioned bloomers?")

Entitled in turn, parents smiled at our
perpetuation of the name, as they moved from the effective
to the dignified in the family's constitution,
lavishing the little kindnesses, the hidden complicities;
and once in awhile thrilling at their reach
over a generation, if a proud grandson should creep home
to show them a gasping trout hooked secretly
from the garden stream of a cordially dislike neighbour.

After their own translation, comes a length
the final act, when we lift to the news of our child's
approaching child already waving in the early scan,
and we must now busk the stage that filial piety requires,
until the last migration to that other Newfoundland where
grandparents have gone before us.

FIRST GRANDCHILD

Fat gold watch, indeed: perfect
miniature, your spring wound up
but three hours since, already
your hands tell us to count each
blessing, measure the future
by your forward direction.
Compact little half-hunter,
whose welcome chirrup signals
no alarm, whose face finds time
for life from moments of love.

SIGHTING

The night Mars passed closer in orbit
to us than it had for 60,000 years,
I took my grandson out to the huge sky
at the mature age of five weeks
to instruct him in the ways of the heavenly bodies.

His focus, let us admit, was at best blurred,
he had slight trouble keeping his concentration,
head lolling, eyes like shooting stars,
his cry was altogether more down to earth:
it was 2 a.m., and he'd lost the milky way.

I told him binoculars enhanced the red
and the bird-scope brought it out like a moon:
he was not impressed, but he made the point for me
that despite the galaxies' expanding dome,
the greatest wonder of all was close at hand.

MOVING WITH *THE TIMES*

The clue for 20 across (7) reads
'How the past differs from the present'.
Ask Arthur Byrant & Malcolm Muggeridge,
whose Course on Democracy sounds intense.
Run a finger down the agony column:
note calls for unwanted artificial teeth.
£12 for Thucydides mint condition,
for rheumatism, colonic irrigation.

I see a lady wishes to dispose
privately of her Rolls-Royce Phantom
and that her chauffeur's 'open for engagement'
(a garage with telephone is also free).
Perhaps she'll use the proceeds to acquire
the A.R.P. garden trench shelter –
a dozen dwarf Michaelmas daisies make
immense cushions, lilac, mauve or blue.

Next page the Lord Chancellor giving judgement
says the question is what does the word 'proportion' mean.
Revue's non-stop at the Windmill Piccadilly;
'*Wild Oats*' is playing at The Prince's.
Frost being less severe in the Vale of Evesham,
the asparagus crop has escaped damage.
In Saskatchewan drought-stricken farmers
send messages along their wire fences.

Obituaries marked the death of Schaliapin.
General Franco's troops have resumed
their advance to the sea. Allied experts
discuss the future size of battleships.
One hundred and forty-seven successive loops
have set a new record for a glider.
The RAF has vacancies for pilots.
Time-bomb explosion kills two in Haifa.

The ayes and noes have tied in the Commons.
The Member of Hexham said the motion only
added to Arab fears in Palestine:
The Speaker cast his vote for the Bill
extending citizenship there to migrants.
The Stock Market remains mostly steady.
I notice pure silk hailspot foulard is
used for a charming new frock from Debenhams.

Mothers are warned to keep babies from air
raid demonstrations. The pelts of Russian
dyed ermine making perfectly fitting boleros.
Conquer your nerves! Write for the free book.

My birth day puzzle makes no fitting sense
for who would understand the human state –
the clues today differ only in tense
from 13 April 1938.

FIFTY YEARS ON
(For Sal)

We still disagree about the exact moment:
whether the pews or the football terraces had it
and who spotted who first
in the smoky light of a Bristol afternoon.
Somehow we had fallen to walking together
and talking. I couldn't believe my luck at this turn
in what they'd arranged as a working weekend,
away from starched collars and straw boaters,
to see how the 'other half' lived in an urban parish,
courtesy of a fiery young priest called Mervyn.

The challenge in your glance seemed to signal,
beneath a hair-style borrowed from Dora Marr
'Come on then, let's see what you're made of.'
Shyly exchanging addresses, I went back to school
hugging the biggest secret since the creation.
My early poems for you were in Latin couplets
because I hardly dared say it in English.
We both know now it was love at first sight,
but for thirteen years I reckon like a Ptolemy
before it dawned my orbit centred on you.

Random comings and goings replayed the journey
over Dartmoor to your sick-bed on my motorbike,
all skids and lost bearings under changing weather.
We each followed our own giddy diversions –
Nancy, Madrid, Dubrovnik; New York, and Hong Kong
where your delicate cast brought its fish to the rise:
at the end of your line to friends, that photograph
they casually played before me over the table
like a well presented mayfly – I took it away
and knew from that instant love could be a decision.

You stepped off the plane in your emerald coat,
and I saw this time it was real. Beneath two trees
in a Somerset lane you embraced me with your answer.
The day of our wedding I crossed the Avon Gorge

not even feeling Brunel under my feet
and still treading air when Bishop Mervyn pronounced
us man and wife in the name of St Matthew Moorfields.
The de luxe dinner at Park's was £7.
Next morning we lifted off to China, joining
Li Po's journey of life, and 'sailing sunward'.

The Ming tower's armilla stood for our course
amid the din and garlic of the Peking air
and Red Guard madness raging like a Gobi dust-storm.
As the Embassy burned, the mob's blows only served
to temper your mettle. We lived and loved through it all
behind our moon-gate entrance in Sweet Rain Alley
or skating by floodlight in the Bei Hai
or hunting on bikes for a piece of yellow rosewood.
Leaving at last the blue-roofed Temple of Heaven,
did we imagine that echo of an unborn cry?

They came with a flurry, the children. I'd forgotten
how hard it was for you in enacting the dutiful
mother and diplomat's wife; and how we had to
make our own beer, knead bread, and wait for the next
foreign post to recoup. From the surgeon's slab
to a career-on-the-rocks you never complained.
Our squalls blew themselves out, like Aprils of tears
washing an iris sky to the full prism
(no nimbus bruise on our horizons flagging
the late low troughs which nearly drowned us all).

Why did I always think of mandrake root
whenever we waved them off from another airport
or wrenched our life to a new peregrination,
kids growing taller in the surf, each parting
a small bereavement, which albums do not show
in the galloping carousel of summer holidays?
For you it was harder, the serial letting-go,
the vacant phases. Now, 'standing on their own feet'
they each returned to us with handsome interest
your long investment of love from the beginning.

If life is opera, our curtain rose on Rossini –
the garrulous passion, the huge crescendi always
resolved in the major; then it was *Intermezzo*
or *Capriccio*, music and words interlaced
to weave from their filigrees of conversation
a sure intimacy that brought us through
all that epic folderol of public life
(the Don Magnificos the betrayals and disguises)
to follow instead the whisper of our glade-boat
parting the diamond waters of the Okavango.

The kernel of our love now, is it this
constant surprise of gradualness, growing
like quilts or needlepoint, the Thonet chair's rattan
you peg in strip by strip, the indoor winter
seed-dibbling, the simmering brew of oranges
that cools in jars to prick the air with kumquat;
and our garden beyond, taking on the seasons,
where you bend to the shifting tapestry of greens,
faithful to your own Ithaca, as each spring
our magnolia chases night with a thousand candles?

That recent summer's day off Druidson,
Skomer on the skyline, waves on fire with light,
a camera caught us walking out of the sea,
hands linked, a spring in our step, as if
just baptised by Botticelli's Venus.
That's how I feel with you still.
Backlit
by a crouching sun, the snapshot stages us
kicking over our shadows' lengthening reach
while the little breakers behind shuffle us on,
and love's tide keeps flooding up the beach.

[See cover of *At A Tangent* for the photo.]

from *Chasing the Hoopoe* (2005)

THE SLIP

Do you recall that day on the clinker, when
pitching from Carrigillihy over to
      Seal Island stretched out on the skyline,
  suddenly we saw the waves get higher?

How can we joke at what we were risking, with
children so small and no-one to notice our
      plight from up on the gorsy headland,
  Sullivan's boat shipping slaps the water?

Near misses, each remembers a later one:
car hurtling backwards (a burst) on the motorway;
      knife at the throat in Spain; the last gasp
  life-saving help from a Transkei rip-tide,

medal awarded. What do you make of it?
Should we insure all risks, should we hire a good
      lawyer, or contact Health & Safety,
  hoping there might be a claim to trade on?

Danger can teach how to trust. Fragility
rules. I could fall tomorrow. Today I still
      bless return to a sloping jetty,
our summer days at *'The Slip'* to launch them.

TAKING DOWN THE CARDS

Night with her train of stars
falls on the frozen landscape of Kanski,
foundling girls at prayer in the chapel
gaze out over Barnes pond in winter.

Picasso's dove of peace
peeps from beneath clementine and cranberry
beyond grasp of the volunteer teaching
a mother's group knitting in Dhankuta Nepal.

And here's the Reverend Dr Robert Walker again
skating on Duddingston Loch, heading straight for
the 1434 adoration of the kings
by way of bitterns and the RSPB.

Scrimshaw from distant soundings,
prayer-flags for the household gods,
almanac moonshine,
they deal me a concealed hand
a flush. I watched for insinuation
of the *tarocchi*, the Wheel of Fortune
in flourished greetings, round robins.

Till next year, I play them as they fall,
push the game to the limit,
let it build a precarious
ziggurat of words and images,
lasting no longer than
the next breath.

IMAGE

The dwarf lilac bush
is bouncing with long-
tailed tits
doing a jig
for the first day of spring

Behind the window
my cat Boyo sits
in a Zen hush
his jaws snapping
like elastic bands
one paw

clapping.

SNOW BUNTINGS AT FLOYD BENNETT FIELD

Brooklyn's old, ocean-edge runway
is lit with toadflax,

the horizon's bare of kettlepond, fence-reeds,

quahog, horseshoe-crab
do not reach,

no hawk marks
semiquavers in the air,

no bush
harbours the confusing fall warbler.

Dead low of the faded year.

They are like
memories scattering but when

those white scraps
blow skittering across forgotten tracts

I zoom all eye, clear
them quick for take-off,

with their named blessings
return to Manhattan's hotspot

not fretting.

UPWELLINGS

To wake from antediluvian sleep,
Cyclopean eyelids would blink heavy in the grass:
saddlebacks wet with garúa mist
inch their hinged domes through the upland pasture
of Santa Cruz.

Afloat on the Humboldt swell, I browse
the pages of a rare edition, for the moment
when Europe's storm-clouds and *Zarathustra*
launched the wistful Germans out of their dreams
in the Tiergarten, toward errant landfall
on the pitch-lava boulders of Floreana.

'Nourmahal 1932' – cliff-face graffiti
fix that visit of Vincent Astor's yacht,
when he dined the Crusoe pair on board.
Sally Lightfoots, who danced clear
of his menu, still scamper fire-red
over the rocks, as if straight from the pot,
to be skewered on the night-heron's bill.

The courtliness of boobies is prelapsarian:
marking time, they lift then lower in turn
each sky-blue, webbed foot, like a priest
laying hands to bless; and proffer ritual twigs
to complete the minuet. Frigate-birds puff
their gullets into balloons of vermilion bubblegum
ruminate the next act of aerial piracy.

When I dive with sea-lions
and greet the submarine penguin,
I am not thinking of fumaroles, or
the sea floor spreading in subduction of continents.

The antics of damselfish with the manta ray's
rippling coverlet distract me from the pulse
of hotspots in the deep mantle, the rising
and falling tide of earth's magma core.
A flightless cormorant semaphores with ragged stumps
that one must learn the hard way.

Basalt contours on the shoreline resolve into
basking heaps of marine iguana, who raised
mohican crests and spit salt. I wonder at days
reflected on a white sand scored only
by the aboriginal calligraphy of sea turtles
en route to bury their eggs. Everywhere such fecundity,
such animal indifference to man,
despite his pillage, puzzled even Darwin.

Giant prickly pears lend their noon shade
to relief of the carpenter bee.
Beyond the trifid mangroves, flamingos
suck water-boatmen from lagoon ooze.
At evening the short-eared owl takes post
on Genovesa's lava field, ready to ferret
the storm petrels' young from their holes.
Night moths alight to inflame the blossoms
of candelabra cactus. As darkness falls on the equator,
bottlenose dolphins patrol the islands,
luminous in the cold upwelling.

A SONG OF PRAISE

Neither the scarlet macaw or the blue-crowned motmot,
nor the white-tipped reef-shark gliding under my flippers;
not the boa in his tree hole beside the Sierpé River,
nor yet, on her delicate egg cup, the violet sabre-wing
humbles me, as these marshalled Lilliputians.

For their trails mark the rainforest floor; and they climb up trees.
For their route measures ten cricket pitches; it is clear as a bike track.
Lo, they move ceaselessly through the humus, and up into the canopy:
their traffic goes orderly to and fro, keeping left like the English.
From the tree-tops they crop their crescent-shaped harvest;
their soldiers' bite can cut leather.

I am breathless with wonder at the order of their cosmos.
Their caravan flows like a munchkin river; their caravels inspire torrents of haiku.
Their leaf loads are a flutter of green sails: like wind-surfers they topple and
    recover balance.
They hold banners upright above their backs; and steer by the pheromones.
Kubla Khan's horsemen boasted fewer flags: Agamemnon's phalanx, fewer shields.
Should I drag a London bus by my teeth? My strength and pride are brought low.

Red spoil lies in tons over their vaulted nests: the chambers of their colonies
    are legion.
Let me follow their tunnels deep to the roots; their entrances go down to the
    citadel.
Let me bow to their Queen, the winged victory: in the lek,
she subdues seven males; her offspring are myriad.

Let me number their dark farms in fathoms; and their workers in millions.
For compost they lay down their loads, to nourish their sacred fungus:
they husband the bloom of its milky filaments; they wait on mycelium.
For this is their manna, the bread that the Lord has given them:
this is their cult; and their manner of cultivation.

Rouse them not to wrath. Their diggings hobble the cattle;
with their catacombs they sap foundations of buildings.
In life they take double tithe from each year's forest growth:
in death they bequeath their jaws as sutures for open wounds.
O let us not in our foolishness turn away from such lore:
let the butterfly not dazzle us with electric blue.
For they and their scattered tribes already outnumber mankind;
and leaf-cutter ants shall inherit the earth.

HOMAGE TO A GOVERNMENT
(September 2002. After Philip Larkin)

Next year we are to send the soldiers off
with moral fervour, and this is all right.
The place from World War One we got bogged down in
we now have fewer men to get bogged down in.
Crusades are meant for sending soldiers off:
in Palestine they seem to work all right.

It's hard to say who wanted it to happen.
As for the rule of law, nobody minds:
'To save successors from the scourge of war'
didn't mean Arabs really. And the war,
provided something awful doesn't happen,
may help to get Al Qaeda off our minds.

Next year our soldiers may invade the country
we founded once in post-War moral fervour
(and other tyrants can expect the same).
At home, with luck, things will be much the same.
But tell our children we're a lesser country
when common sense is ruled by moral fervour.

STILL LIFE IN NEW YORK

I.

With orchards in '*Le Périgord*'
delicate as petticoats
assume that elevated pose
of ballerinas,

their five blossoms and two unburst
lime-green buds
holding the empty restaurant's rapt attention
for the last distilled
moments of silence, until

Manhattan's garrulous lunch-hour unleashes
its vegetable onslaught,
and the dance resumes.

II.

The small Attic wine-jug,
red on black terracotta,
mid fifth century BC,
depicts the young man leaving
for that war in which the sons of Oedipus
contended for the throne of Thebes
and he would be killed.

Already armed with spear and shield,
his tunic neatly pleated, he receives
from his mother's outstretched hands
the plumed helmet
that was to cover his fashionable curls
for the last time.

In sunlight from a Fifth Avenue window
the intent figures
move still among the motes,
perfectly describing a world's circle
to which no poetic line
is more than a tangent.

THE SHILLINGED BIRCHES
   ('There is only the fight to recover what has been lost')

As the school-bus took the corner, wind lifted
the birch tree branches, shifting the light's angle.
Leaves shimmied in the sun, a heavenly jackpot
cascading a rush of shillings through green air.

That first lucid exposure, undeveloped
from the dark cells, emerged to no solution,
its figure only recurring as a reminder
down the long divisions of fifty years.

Others followed, each chance illumination
(say cutting a stick, or stepping over a stream)
held the singularity of the split second
in a sharp image whose quick I longed to reach.

Such flashes gone, their pungent drift would linger
like smoke over a conjuror's empty hat,
the watcher sensing his pockets begin to bulge
with the improbable doves. It was a trick

not turned, but visited on the open
mind at intervals, off guard, unawares:
a peep behind the curtain of unknowing,
a sudden flame flare from an alternate world.

INVITATION
(Catullus Carmen XIII)

Dear Fabullus,
               You will dine well at my place
this coming weekend, if our stars stay lucky,
provided you bring with you the wherewithal
of a good menu, bring also the bottles,
salt up your jokes, and don't forget the popsy.
If, old friend, you arrive equipped with all this,
you'll have a good meal. As for me (Catullus)
I find my wallet's filled only with cobwebs.
But in return I promise love's cocktails neat,
and, to show we're cool and still in the fast lane,
you may try the bouquet of *my* girl's perfume,
her own luxury 'Aura Amorosa'.
Once you've scented those pheromones, you will wish
Nature could make you one one huge proboscis!

MAY LANE, BIRMINGHAM
    (after *Gardeners' World*)

His coriander shooting green tongues,
over his rake Mohammed Ali says
people who do allotments aren't made.

Bean-sticks, bird scarers, plastic bottles
stake out these patchwork acres where
you follow string straight down the rows

or skip a sort of ballerina hop-scotch
from one to another, not surprised to see
rumps rear up like errant cantaloups.

Jahangir Singh navigates with care
to nurse his crop of marrows and courgettes
as one who ferries souls to their salvation.

Whipping thoroughbred race-horse manure
to curds of liquid amber guarantees
Thomas's dahlias beat all the odds.

While Arthur sticks to planting Kestrel spuds,
for gooseberry juice calypso-style Cynthia
spikes her mix with Guinness on the spot.

Asked Teresinha how she grows colours,
fermenting leaves to bleed wode on cloth
dipped to deepen bluer under daylight –

they are like photographs developing:
Friends discovered clutching their first fruits –
a perfect set, growing together, laughing.

ELIZABETH'S VERSION

I could wish, brother, more poetry in him,
less theatre. To scotch Valentines to a whim,
how childish. He thinks I pray at Saint Olave's
just for the dancing master? Look how I slave
all the year round – I doubt that enters into
his crotchety short-hand. And it's no sin to
lift French minuet above *cazzo dritto*.
I love him, but he risks my love's memento
engrossed with hot tong where they cut out his stone.
'Prick-louse' must change his tune, or trill to atone!

Stomachful? Yes, I put it all down to fear
the ancient name might founder without an heir.
His bobbin threadless, how could I close the stitch?
So, plagued by his own pest, fired by an itch
to fumble every skirt, he would gad about
like some perriwigged Polcinello, played out,
mocked from the quarterdeck. Then pity whispered
'The heart may soon grow sick when hope is deferred:
bolder jointure is easy for your beauty
to conceive – call it a catholic duty.'

His fishmonger uncle has already asked
to sire my child for gold (what cod!). But the task
was now to catch seed blown from farther afield,
to spring home-grown. With a birth, I knew he'd yield
and his lion be caged. To Brampton by coach
I fell in with a King's Guard man, whose approach
brought back at once the Lambeth gypsy's riddle
'Fortune's messenger will not ride side-saddle'.
We broke the day's passage at The Reindeer Inn.
By candle, many would have been taken in.

A small bird fluttered, and I rejoiced to hide
belly in billowing morning gown. Outside
Dutch ships sailed up the Thames, and the press of war
kept him as distant as the evening star.
I never told him. But when I lost the child,
feigning simply my months had returned, he smiled
as if some gibbous thought half-formed in his mind,
then turned back to prospects of The Golden Hand
and Navy business. As I have since turned back
to painting Our Saviour, and my sun is black.

(Elizabeth de St Michel, wife of Samuel Pepys, died on 10 November 1669 at the age of 29, and was buried in Saint Olave's Church, Hart Street)

PEKING RAP

I.

The Queen's messenger was late. A mob at the gate
had swelled all morning. Another warning
never got through: friends knew
something was afoot – lads on foot
with full jerry-cans spelled plans.
Telephone cut, couldn't get out –
sentries: 'Don't, or China won't
be responsible'. Quite impossible
not to laugh, so we didn't half-
roar at the Peter Sellers movie.
Off-screen, suddenly, it was moving:

II.

Our man's just bid three-no-trumps
when the night roars back, and we catch a glimpse
of a Verey flare as a surge of bodies
over the wall floods up towards us,
'THEY'RE COMING IN!'
followed by the din
of pole-axed doors, burst windows:
shock—, blitz—, bangs—, blows!
The twenty-three of us trapped alone
fall back fast to the strong-room zone,
while ten thousand light the flame
for their once-in-a-lifetime bonfire game,
and the Lion & the Unicorn's sole defence
pleads *honi soit qui mal y pense*.
Sparks leap up, smoke gets thicker,
breath in this small room comes quicker;
stuff gushes through the window bars,
Red Guard shouting 'sha! sha!'
(better not translate for the ladies)
Fire now rages, hot as Hades,

bricks cave in as a pile drives through,
(might get stuck if the door jams to).
Some of us wonder: is this moment
how we'll know our final moment?
Out we stagger to the screaming mass
of our fellow-creatures having a gas
as they gouge and punch and twist and tear,
and somebody's pulling out my wife's hair,
and someone else rips off her pants,
lewd prying fingers leave their prints,
my teeth bite deeper into his arm,
down we go to the stinging swarm.
Our man floats off with a blood-drenched face.
While we're locked in hate's embrace,
arc lights glare and a camera whirrs
to shoot us live, and their *cri de guerre*'s
'Tell your crimes and bow your head
you English dogs, or you'll be dead!'

III.

One of us did die not long after,
another lay motionless for weeks,
one went mad for a year. Laughter
was not why it hurts to speak.

Now, as I hear the spool unwind
my distant, dated, plummy voice,
this brush with danger sounds small beer
compared with those who'd had no choice:

the millions who the Great Leap Forward
starved to death for a Party phrase;
the millions who'd been 'rectified'
or suicide cut short those days;

a nation's children who we watched
forfeit their school years and their youth,
for whom denouncing parents was
the recommended way to truth.

I bow to China and her beauty,
and hold no grudge, just this conclusion
let Mao be judged by history,
and f___ all bloody revolution!

(On 22 August 1967, a Red Guard mob burned down the British Diplomatic Mission in Peking and beat up its occupants who were prevented from leaving China for the next 18 months)

from *Echo Soundings* (2012)

LOOKING DOWN MACDOUGAL
For Charlotte Johnson Wahl, after her 1991 painting

Cassandra, you have not found it strange
those towers should frame a vanishing point,
while round you buildings tilt and bulge,

like giants spilling from fair-ground mirrors
or waves rebounding up the sky's cliff,
ochre to blood-red in the early sun;

and that at your feet should crowd so many
desolate ash-grey faces, streaming
from sight to escape the precipitation

of fiery impasto, with only the swan's neck
street-lamps standing for residue of hope;
as you signed before the fall.

KENNEDY'S LATIN PRIMER
   i m. Steven Lawn 1972–2001

From cover to cover a lifetime, the long and short of it.
Trouble was, the covers were coming off.
Visiting the old school half a century later
I cadged from the librarian another copy,
used but intact, with borrowers' names inscribed.
My excuse was to coach young Adam, son
of a local Chinese restaurateur in London.

But my shelves would have seemed empty without this
familiar presence to which I occasionally resort
as one does to a summer-house or childhood haunt.
It's good to be reminded that the principal
parts of love remain simple, active or passive,
despite the moods and mixed conjugations of rivals
like seize, entice or avenge.

I'd still rather conjugate than decline,
though you need to know a case when you see one.
The gender-rhymes are a must. I'm also partial
to the semi-deponent verbs, such as dare, trust and rejoice.
But, best of all, the scansion: dashes and little half-moons
scatter the page with confetti, as vowel and syllable
are crowned and take their place in the lyric stanza.

A Lego game to map a model world?
   'The world is everything that is the case'.
A face emerging through a complex grammar?
   'Tomorrow is easy but today is uncharted.'
I think my feeling's nearer what was meant
before the Reformation by the word 'primer' –
a Book of Hours and its illuminations.

And only now for the first time do I spot
that the last borrower's signature on the fly-leaf
is the same name that's carved on Grosvenor Square's
Memorial for the British who fell with the towers –
the only one from my school, less than ten years
after leaving. I take the book in both hands, and try
to construct a conditional clause from the verb 'to hope'.

THE CAKE OF CUSTOM
'...reaching something better' – *Physics and Politics 1872*

For Brian Urquhart

Bagehot throws long shadows
as you walk below
the vaulted arches ('Let the nations rejoice').
But among remaining body parts
you will search hard for the heart
or to hear an honest voice.

Reality, someone said, is a circus tent
carried round, folding, adjustable.
Remember the press photograph
where we witnessed the Peace signature,
back row jostling to be seen, some later biddable
as staff to Prime Minister or President
to advise that the case for war was clear,

as night skies already lit their Big Top?
Ringmasters, you cannot cry stop
once the high wire is slung,
big cats come roaring on,
and splay-footed through the elephant dung,
waving fake bouquets, the clowns flip-flop.
The show's too far gone.

Beguiled by the theatre
of it all, to know what would happen
next ('Why, then, the world's mine oyster,
which I with sword will open')
our illusions grew only deeper.
As also, with time, does the pain

of final recognition,
welling up beneath
the public pulling of teeth
from the Prince's fixed grin,
that the new Machiavelli
and the old Macaroni
are one: and neither dignified nor efficient, for the Constitution's linch-pin

TURING TEST

Before the apple, something understood,
his imitation game, the unlikelihood
sex would remain concealed behind a screen,
chess, his marathons, the ultimate machine…
till dead man's hand, emerging from its box,
flicks *Off*, withdraws, the lid comes down, it locks.

Brief span. He broke the codes to win the War.
Original computer avatar,
he wrestled with the uncomputable
like Jacob with the angel; then took flight,
running life's algorithms to the full –
an Alpha Leonid pencilling the night.

END GAME

The last hours blew up the historic treaty.
Under Moscow's bind over 'crossing the line',
we'd conceded three square brackets on the telephone.
When we met in the Octyábrskaya's whited sepulchre,
our compass was beginning to veer uncertainly;
the word *'verlegt'* triggered open disagreement,
and after further skirmishing we broke.
The upshot was large-scale Russian military manoeuvres
(which the Four Points had specifically excluded);
a door-knock at dead of night put on the frighteners,
and produced the dishevelled form of words by morning,
with running updates on our Toshiba lap-top.
Acrimony, obtuseness and emotion:
I do not wish to exaggerate the achievement.

PAYLOAD

Departing New York's carpeted shadows
as suits of light jousted over Cuba,
he'd never found the nearest shelter.

Caught since in the middle-game, he used
a sabbatical among departed souls
to bone up on the variations;

entered the mountain, silos, submarines,
found a priesthood worthy of pyramids,
a set of axioms leading somewhere.

His rolodex bristled with acronyms,
warhead numbers, target options,
all their 'circular errors probable'.

You need to have acted Prime Minister
in the Whitehall bunker, he told me once,
to know how it felt when our double agent

suddenly warned us the other side
took our latest nuclear play for real,
and had moved to First Strike Alert.

He remembered nearly coming to blows
at Pinter's jibe – You parrot that stuff
because you're paid to. Now it all seemed

much less certain, or was it just
the usual erosions of age? He'd watched
some recent hearings on TV

where a younger man deployed his brief
with the same smooth assurance. We agreed
that keeping each envelope sealed containing

the key had been dearly won by those
who'd survived two wars; but that no-one knew
the endings for n-dimensional chess.

RECEPTION

You enter the room
as if emerging on stage
trying to recall
which of the many bit-parts
must be resumed this evening.

The alpha males bray
to each other. The ladies
affect to listen
while searching beyond, but turn
aside from the also-ran.

This is what we can't
admit: in front or behind,
to move in any
circle traces the same nought,
the painted *Merry-Go-Round*.

I wish the rule was:
speak only verse, sign-language,
or a foreign tongue
stipulated in advance
on the RSVP card.

TABLE TALK
    'Sir, the insolence of wealth will creep out'

Strange, the very rich
often talk much, ask little,
in conversation
they seem to claim for themselves
the right to be listened to.

As if no other
measure could bring dividend,
could yield interest.
This blithe self-estimation
explains why heads were once lopped.

Over Glyndebourne's lawn
I hear one of two women
on his arm asking
"And *sine qua non* is what?"
The *Don*'s last hand-shake, my dear.

SKEP

Half a merrythought, the scop's wishbone;
skipjack jump off Cape Cod; tub for the pit-horse;
bucket, basket, or cage; water-wheel scoop;
villain's pocketful of money; coal scuttle;
age-long scope for lip work – not love's labour
or vain repetition of prayer for something lost,
but ells of straw coiled and bound in split
briar strips, laced with a bone awl, wound
over cow-horn girth, to raise the domed grace
of finished skep, decked out with eke and hackle,
which took and housed whole centuries of swarm,
and still gives off the buzz that keeps us warm.

COLUMELLA'S NIPPLE

'the wax cell where the royal offspring is raised
is easy to see at the edge of the comb, proud
like the nipple of a breast'. – *De Re Rustica Bk IX*

Lonely on the Loeb shelf,
scarlet and gold, but not taking yourself
too seriously. Quick to poke fun
at old Virgil's poetic licence
in turning from common sense
to give the fable another run

that swarms have spontaneous birth
from the carcass of an ox, tongue in cheek
you note the death-rate of bees
falls short of requiring such a top-heavy approach.
Yours is a vintage critique
from the working farmer's eye, down-to-earth,
with none of an armchair expert's urge to preach.

It feels like some mesolithic
rock painting, where I'm one of those tiny stick-
figures swaying on roped esparto
up a sheer face to hunt for wild nest
honey; and half-way there I see you
ahead of me by twenty centuries, as you pick
deftly among the combs, handing down the best.

READING ALOUD
   For Jane Duran

The words are pacing
themselves, are not out of breath.
Notice how your voice
becomes somebody else's,
the room larger than before.

Practise each morning,
moving along the bookshelf.
The chairs will sit up
sensing a change in the air.
Every day sounds different.

No need to force things
open the bindings and let
the poems take light;
even catch a refracted
glimpse of your own other self.

COMING DOWN TO EARTH
i.m. Jim Cogan, English teacher and founder of youth charities in Africa

Grief, like happiness, fulfills itself
shared. Last supper or wedding party,
no need for competition – doors open
on a starry sky, everyone able
to book-mark their own love's place
before loss or the wrong ending.

Just as my pre-dawn dream is ending,
you appear again, your old self
knowing death but anxious to place
each friend at some reunion party,
lighter now than when you were able
to carry me bodily over the open

Lympstone fields. Fifty years re-open
as I circle round for the right ending,
the personal handful of earth, unable
to find the words I need for myself.
You'd not, I know, be party
to such 'nonsense'. But it has its place.

Our cairn on Mount Ida could have been the place:
let that huge lammergeier open
its coped wings and our shepherd be party
(with his incense) to the rite's ending.
The burning bush will speak for itself
zippo-ed, before the freezing cold disables.

You, like Walcott, were not able
to 'choose between this Africa' (your place)
'and the English tongue' loved for itself –
his *Far Cry* poem (lying here open)
you sent me from Jamaica, ending
your fling with the merchant prince's party.

Ariel or Prospero? You're either party,
out of the cloven pine able
to call young spirits from school's ending
to a new start, Africa being the place
where you led so many to become open
to the gift of generosity itself.

Your place will be kept at any party
where doors open and the young mind's able
by itself (like you) to seek a better ending.

PUTTING THE HEART TO SCHOOL

How does one measure the risk of falling in love
with a place? We have probably all seen it happen,
or felt the parting wrench: a founder letting go
of some prized new creation, the epic voice
above Isaldwana silenced with a shot, the farewell
of a Mr Chips from lessons that have spelled a life-time.

The Abbey chimes another day to life. Time
for would-be new boys to sit and be tested on our love
of irregular verbs. Whether we've fared well
buff telegrams will reveal later. When I happen
to score with the lucky ones it's as if a voice
whispers "Here is the race's starting-line. Now, go!"

Five summers long, the butterflies come and go.
Will the cane sting? Did the ringside bell call time?
Is this a dress rehearsal? Shall I find a voice?
'Odi et amo' said Catullus: and if it were love
would that first kiss in the Abbey be how it would happen?
Or is growing-up learning to strip a Bren gun well?

But 'all shall be well, and all manner of thing shall be well'.
Slowly we found we did not want to let go
of lines remembered or books that might make things happen
to put the world to rights in our own life-time.
Friends were for always. Masters taught us to love
the Idea for itself. We shouted the hymns with one voice…

not always hearing the few who would quietly voice
their loneliness, or a sense of loss that the 'Well
of Life' would never quite assuage. Should one un-love
a place for that? Not I, for whom leaving was letting go
of a father I'd never had, after the time
of my life: without which, the rest couldn't have happened.

So I came back to School to learn how it happens
fifty years on, when we reinvent the voice,
the music to set old values to modern time.
A risky call, to venture "All's fair, all's well";
Safer no doubt to stick to "Steady as we go".
But feel the generosity, feel the love!

We recognise a farewell when it happens:
Letting go is easier once you find the voice
to express a love that has lasted almost a lifetime.

LITHIUM

    In 1948 the Australian psychiatrist John Cade discovered the medical properties of $Li^2 Co^3$

Take from the table atomic
number three, it is worth a mass.
Imagine an altar, the proffered
wafer, where we kneel humbly
before the lucent alkali, accept
a stone as bread. The reredos
depicts a raging fire quenched,
Black Dog in slumber.

Three times in one decade
through a dark wood
we've all skirted the abyss,
and blessed our guide John Cade –
'Write an ode to him' you said, 'someone should':
I love the hint of metal in your kiss.

EXERCISE
For Mimi Khalvati

I'd write a poem every day
to help the dopamine along
if I knew all I had to say.

The best lines happen on the way
to somewhere else they don't belong.
I ran around the Park today,

it sparked a random roundelay,
with jackdaws joining in my song
as if they knew what it would say.

In workshops I have tried to play
poetic scales – when they went wrong
returned to try another day;

I've even played the castaway,
or sat beside a billabong
hearing what the Dreamings say.

In the end you can't sashay
(the life so short, the Art so long).
Just write the poem every day
and learn what *it* has had to say.

SERENGETI

From couch grass
hackled tussocks
a cheetah rises
nonchalant as death

outstares a rampant
sun   jaw levelled to
the plain's horizon
the yawning day

where multitudes
of nodding beards
pursue their exodus
toward the season's

promised waters
filling the air with
monotone amens

Ambles   veering
quickens toward
the lifeline   liquid
shoulder-blades lifting

till all chicane
elided   the bright
shadow stretches

svelte
full pelt
veld

dealt

African grace
amen   amen

IN THE PALM HOUSE

Beached spaceship under morning dew,
a crepitation in the warm, damp air.
Return ticket to another planet.

A quarter-millennium in touch with Kew,
they are trying to signal – *Look up, tune in,*
these benign sentinels – *for upon it*

may hang survival. A fishtail palm
is poised to eject straight through the roof;
the bark code reads – Few years, no re-count.

Confabulation in green. Frond language:
raffia to rattan, henna to mahogany,
babassu to neem. Somehow you can't

escape the feeling they are filling time
we should not let slip. The starfruit whispers
that peepul has given up on Buddha.

Corkscrew climb to the skywalk. On the bridge,
a final supplication of leaves (umbrella,
shuttlecock). From here, I begin to perceive better

nature's life-span, the whole launch and heave
of growing things. Their lift-off, uplift.

New Poems

OMEN

Out of the blue
by our French windows
landed a grey heron
on the garden table,
peered through long enough
then gave us all up
and away.

Few days later,
a still warm song thrush
lay motionless by the same doors.
Sun reflecting the garden
on closed windows, the bird
had fallen for it. Such beautiful feathers –

l almost missed the pinhead
of blood from his beak.

PASTORAL

The wood mouse is a dainty chap,
He trotteth to and fro.
At noon he often takes a nap
To keep his pulse-rate low.

He sets great store by etiquette
His coat gives off a sheen.
His whiskered jaw he'll never let
Be anything but clean.

Flowerbeds are his favoured hides
As evening shadows fall.
My house he's doubtful of; besides
The step is much too tall.

One night two tabbycats pass by.
'Can we give you a lift?'
Wary, the mouse makes no reply….
But can't refuse the gift.

They entertain, they spare no pains,
Then offer him some more.
And in the morning, there remains
Just half a whiskered jaw.

ALCAICS FOR BRUBECKS

Here is a landscape Horace would recognise,
two thousand years have made little dent on it
or on the life of contadino
save that now tractor displaces oxen.

Evergreen holm-oak, cypress and poplar re-
echo the unrelenting cicada, while
olive and fig and purple cluster
ripen to mark the recurring season.

Daily by high noon these terraced walls become
furnaces, daily the evening breezes
fold with sheep-bells their tide of coolness
into a pattern of Tuscan fresco.

Shade of Catullus, for supper bring only
shaved pecorino, pasta, carpaccio,
served with a Montisi brunello
fit for the verses of Roman poets.

Leaving, we pour libations to Grigio's
magical presence, cull mint and fennel,
pray Colombaio's household gods that
all remain thus per aeterna saecla.

MOMENTS

O almost extinct
salmon-crested cockatoo
your eye sees through us

out of the river
mayfies fan the evening air
gathering swallows

autumn shadows fall
the passion flower lights up
its little lanterns

a pebble in the palm
pulls the body down to earth
gravid stoniness

LAYING QUEEN
(Her lion-red body, her wings of glass – Sylvia Plath)

The best of the photographs I ever took
was in the garden by my opened hive,
bar one, we'd gone through all the frames – then, look!
surrounded by workers, the Queen was much alive.
She had just settled rump-down on the next cell
to lay an egg whose sex she would always know,
but the workers all broke up and she could tell
from the sudden burst of light it was time to go.

The 91st Honey Show (as they say "We serve mankind")
had given the photo FIRST PRIZE on a scarlet card;
the Queen (now framed behind glass) didn't seem to mind
and buyers of honey crowded the Club's back-yard.

MALUS HUPUHENSIS IN APRIL

We brought it just as a sapling
to live in our new garden.
Twenty years later the tree rules all.

Its spring mantle of white blossom
speaks in the breeze, and has taught us
who presides over the lawn.

A completely white dove flew in
today to join the greys searching
for fallen nyger-seeds from a feeder

The tree's loose girth is almost three feet long,
Its top is higher than our bedroom windows
Its overall shape is like a world-globe
made up of leaves and flowers

My bees are still all over this tree's delicate flowers
catching up on pollen and nectar after cold winds
The old red maple is an arboreal friend
though the two of them never touch

GETTING THE BIRD
(For Wendy Cope)

I went on Amazon the other day
to re-stock on a book that's out of print.
Used or remaindered, had no more to pay
than postage (plus one penny). Didn't stint

but took the lot. They drop in one by one
from different corners. Gives me quite a boost
that all these poems now can be re-run.
So far ten *Hoopoes* have come home to roost.

And what is more, the history of some
is shown by my inscription on the fly.
So I can tell which friends remain a chum
and where it's best to let such matters lie.

BIRTHDAY VILLANELLE

Darling, it doesn't seem so long,
Since first we stepped the dinner-dance.
At eighty years you're still 'on song'.

My love for you remains as strong
As when you shot the fateful glance
It really doesn't seem so long.

And you were right and I was wrong,
That mountain wasn't worth the chance.
You're eighty now: we're still on song.

The young ones to whom you belong
Embrace you as the years advance
In their lively, loving throng.

And that is why you must prolong
Your lead role in our family dance,
(As 'Mem' does with our Aussie throng.)

The stars have blessed us all along:
Each family marks a renaissance.
At eighty years you're still 'on song' –

Though we no longer have so long!

SONNET
For my wife after 50 years

A love-song is the hardest to engender
beyond the midway point. This paradox
does not predict an absence of things tender,
though still the less of turning back the clocks.
The art of jewelled words seems overdone,
it's the shared life requires the artistry.
Remember Jonson's tribute to his son:
the children are our love's best poetry.

So I shall not repeat my boyhood odes
and fresh poetics are not mine to lead.

But look, the garden's sudden passion-flowers
light up their little fruits like autumn codes
which, to the bees and us, deciphered read:
our love renews each year like April showers.

CHINESE

Hangs from my wall
a calligraphy gift
from my old teacher
in epitaph style of
the Later Han period

"Words   Love
teach   shows
good   the
nature   divine"

Mao's own grass-hand
sparked no prairie fire of
more enduring revolution.

SLOW LIGHT BURNING
   (For John Mole)

Physicists say it's the easier way
for burning a spectral hole,
and open anew their Universe view:
with reality's frontier as goal.

The world is a mess. Even Mao knew that,
in his poem for Li Shu-yi.
Then let's stay off the moon, where it's far too soon
to take nuclear heat for the tea.

Back where I started, alight are those words,
and look for a trigger to fire them.
If the slow light burns on, and the lyrics grow strong,
someone may even admire them.

FROM SHORT POEMS BY SHI TAO
    (my translation requested by Amnesty International)

I forget all
language starts
from the simplest words

Memory like a lamp
in the slave's hand
kneeling, I beg it to last

Night moves on inch
by inch. Before dawn's first
light I search for a life

No news of a boat
mooring alongside
Over my face

A sea breeze plays
its taste is called
sorrow

With doddering hand
I write this painful thing
the gun in my ear

the salt in my spit
and on my hair
the gold

All my life I'm confused
by the same bearings
sand-storm, then curtain up

I dread looking West,
purgatory's ultra-violet
testing my middle years

[Shi Tao poet, journalist and writer was arrested on 24 November 2004 on charges of 'illegally divulging State secrets abroad', because he had notified foreign media contacts of a government directive forbidding commemoration of the Tiananmen massacre. On 27 April 2005 he was sentenced by a Chinese court to 10 years imprisonment. He was released 18 months early of that.]

TROMPE L'OEIL

In Liguria
no one leans from a painted
balcony. The lace
figure in the curtains hides
her breasts like a real angel.

Dickens found fireflies
on the path to Camogli:
I saw peregrines,
a boy with a boom-box, and
purple sea-lungs by the rocks;

picnicked on Swiss chard
quiche and flowering lovage;
swam at Paraggi,
the Berlusconi villa
kept safe by watchdogs in shades.

VILLANELLE
   (Father to Son)

Just set your clock before each night.
When morning comes the day will be
another chance to put things right.

And, yes, it really is alright
to mourn what was not meant to be.
But you must work to make things right.

Letters to friends always delight,
and you'll feel less an absentee
If you write more, to put things right.

Take exercise with all your might,
work all day like the humble bee
and you will then be less affright.

Fear not the Court, the odds seem bright.
One day you will be fit and free,
just keep strait on to make it right

Clouds sometimes hide the sun's true light'
So let this scrap of poetry
 help to alleviate your plight
For Westward look! The land is bright.

JIGSAW

A 'still life' can be misleading, though sometimes
one form may change another, and then

both may benefit from it. Take, for example,
Jacob van Hulsdonck's painting "Oranges and Lemons"

which, centuries later, a much respected
London art dealer used as the model

for a design-led, uniquely cut, wooden puzzle,
which he gave away in large numbers to potential
clients frequenting his art gallery, us included.

I am sure in the covid years
we were not alone in finding great pleasure
from this jigsaw challenge.

And there is still life in our home,
whichever way you look at it!

HAM HOUSE PARTY

Pepys would have loved it –
the style, glitter and pizzazz,
the living statues
greeting guests at the North front,
powdered flunkeys at the South.

Champagne flowing to
strains of Mozart, the marquee
(tented palazzo!),
the sea of tables decked with
flowering candelabra.

"Old friends the most" said
the speeches, amid laughter.
With medals *'For Love'*,
we toasted the half-century,
unveiled 'Laughing Cavalier'.

Then the Royal Marines
(Duke of York and Albany's
1664) marched into the light,
their horns piercing the quick,
and stirring my old Officer's heart.

Finally, firework cannonades
blossomed into the night sky, excelling
the illuminations of Kings.
It was like being
present at the Creation!

For Johnny and Sarah,
what a night to remember!
Four hundred friends all
danced away happy. "Thank you"
we said –
"Pepys would have loved it".

EDWARDES SQUARE
(For My Daughter: On leaving a family flat)

Not those spick Regency terraces
Wrapped in wisteria nodosity,
But a 1940s corner block facing the pub
Beside a world-ash.

A plinth in the hidden gardens
Marks where the barrage balloon had
Anchored through blitz, an errant galleon.
Half a century on

'Buster' too slipped her final moorings
From No. 14; sailed off with her promised
Bostonian key to Elysium, while we
Scattered furtive ashes among the roses.

A boy, stripped to woollen bathing trunks,
I had swayed atop collapsible steps
To distemper ceiling and walls
In the minikin haven
That became her life's space.

Proudly I took there to tea
My first and last love.
The bells Auntie heard ring on;
She was so keen, she set
Your mother and me back years.

In turn she dandled you awkward
Watched by Peynet's porcelain lovers,
The swelling aquamarine roller
Poised in its frame unbearably
To bear us all away.

Once, rusticated from boarding school,
We sent you to her in penance:
You said that loving confinement
Was suffocating.

When she, blind and courageous, faltered,
You followed in, made it home.
New loves flared at the hearth:
Such work and play as were hardly admitted
In 'Science and Health'.

Quitted now after two generations
This threshold recedes into history,
The bronzed deco doorknobs opening
Only to memory.
But for each of you the shared gain,
With her blessing,
May yet sustain
A generation to come.

PESTHOUSE COMMON

We didn't know, when we first took it over,
our corner-house was front seat for history,
while several ploughs were digging up
crocks and glasses from George III's era.

Travellers in June to Epsom Downs
often went through Richmond,
and swerved their caravans off Queen's Road
to rest on the Common. But not this year.

The green ground would barely match a football,
but the blackberry season is a serious race.
Once, sand was laid down the centre
for a flower garden. My bees came fast.

Four giant horse-chestnuts line the road,
the most gigantic is nearest and could take us
with it in an Eastern storm. I drew it
one winter, to understand the risks.

The owls
       are loud at night.
              Foxes are everywhere,
draught horses from
          the Park
are used to mow the Common.
Badgers survive,
           I've seen them.

'LION COUCHANT'
(i m. Boyo 1999–2012)

He leaned slowly over
on to his side
like a last page turning,
his celadon eyes still open
even as his heart stopped
and my own filled with tears.

ONE OF THOSE THINGS

> 'It looms like war, this growing old: we live
> on new frugalities of expectation'
> (from *Embassy* by David Sutton)

Already he was different before it
happened: the Fates were at their looms.
Stress adjustment, psychosis, say what you like,
fuelled by the dark web they brought on war
within himself and with his loved one, and all this
led for one instant to the knife blow, the growing
pool of hurt, the whole family suddenly old
beyond our years. How should we

re-order our lives so that he too can live
again, and his children live on
with the mother and father they love? Does new
hope for us lie beyond the frugalities
permitted by time? I see the end of
this tragedy, through his courage and our enduring expectation.

YEARS GO BY

    'Yes it's not funny... A prisoner told me...
    ...one. in a thousand... will remember'
    (from *Timing* by Michael Donaghy)

Could anyone go down with this illness? Yes,
and at any time. As for hospitals, it's
hit or miss. Though not
as bad as the earlier remand in Wormwood Scrubs. Funny,
they'd moved you to ground level 'for safety'. A
day later an orderly found you on the floor unconscious, then he himself fell
                                                                                                prisoner
to pretence: 'a suicide attempt' was the story they all told...
But your smashed left temple, loss of hearing and of taste, struck a different
                                                                                                            note for me.

There have followed four slow years, in as many hospitals, where not one
could provide the peace for mental healing, in
all that strident, bullying confinement. Instead a
thuggish plunder of your savings by the thousand,
extorted from your bank account with threats of no 'protection'. We will
pass over the NHS blind eye to lodged complaint. But we all still remember.

GOODNESS WILL OUT

    'Don't be afraid old son, it's only me,
    Though not as I've appeared before'
    (from *Haunts* by Michael Donaghy)

Do 'desperate remedies' work? It seems they don't.[*]
In the end children proved to be
what saved you from feeling more afraid.
Love can be young or old,
its very heart for you has been your daughter and your son.
Now carry on despite divorce. So that it's
still both Father and Mother, each doing only
what they do best, without rancour. Seems good enough to me!

An afterthought here perhaps, though?
Grandparents have life experience not
once, but three times over. As
relentless as a grandfather clock, I've
counted things that, on the face of it, appeared
too late, but had the hand not moved, could not have been sounded before.

[*] *Desperate Remedies* – Psychiatry and the Mysteries of Mental Illness' by Professor Andrew Scull (publ. Allen Lane 2022)

AFTERWORD

'The map will follow
each journey you made
to be burdened by history
or promised release'
(from *The Map* by John Mole)

I hardly dare echo the
words. But it's still good to map
going forward and to will
your compass to follow
(with bearings and way points) each
chance you may have for the journey
that can guide you,
and the right decisions can be made.

We are all burdened
one way or another by
the weight of history.
Today ends your 50th year, or
let's just say it crowns your promised
        release.

6 April 2023

GOLDEN JUBILEE SESTINA
(For Ben, 1 June 2002)

Back in the seventies, that was another season –
our house bedecked with bunting, flags in the garden.
At eight and under the children had all the answers,
their fancy dress and street games signalled a journey
whose overture for them was only beginning.
Was it then he heard the call that would echo thereafter?

The dance moved on. It was but a few years after
the Silver, we celebrated the Christmas season
by seeing *Gawain* at the theatre. A small beginning
for him of something enormous – in Covent Garden's
shop for special effects, his foraging journey
furnished a child's quest with real-life answers.

Who knows to what his dramatic instinct answers?
He built a miniature theatre; his play came after,
he called it *The Creation:* God had to journey
through papery stars and a pyrotechnic season,
smoke filled our house and billowed into the garden –
more like the end of the world, than the beginning!

At school, where they taught "In the beginning
was the Word", the word that gave the answers
to him was 'music': it opened a paradise garden
whose colours and mystery gave him what he was after;
young performances blossomed in their due season;
the excitement launched him on to a lifelong journey.

TV became the star-ship for that journey
with its reach through time and space to a new beginning
and wider stage, a technology that can season
grand ideas with racy effects, and answers
his drive to trim every sail both fore and after,
to organise his global digital garden.

Which is how he arrived at Buckingham Palace Garden,
for an early summit in his professional journey
that makes one wonder whatever can follow after
'Prom at the Palace': where, from a simple beginning,
he came up trumps with an evening of golden answers,
a concert to crown the Queen's Jubilee season.

It is good every season to undertake a journey,
a new beginning, without having all the answers.
As for the garden, one can write poems there, after.

BALLAD OF CARRAGILIHY AND INISHBOFIN

On the first day of our holidays
We took the ship to Cork;
Bunk-cabins deep, ten hours to sleep   *The trip out*
And faces white as chalk.
Then farewell *Innisfallen,*
We left your slippery walk
For the rains of Caragillihy
In the West of County Cork.

Oh, excitement to discover
The old house where we're to stay:
Explore the stairs, claim beds, find lairs,   *Arrival*
Run down to smell the bay.
The bowls are rich with strawberries,
The garden's full of hay,
The rose on shells the dawn foretells
Of morrow's endless day.

Ben's the clarion fanfare
That summons all to table;
Gabriel's the jewelled glass   *We*
From necklaces in fable;   *pass*
Rufus rules crab-circus school   *the*
And caterpillar stable;   *time*
And Mummy'd buy that cottage sty
If only she were able!

Rabbit Island still entices
To her caves and shingled sand –
Quick, launch the boat and all afloat   *The boat*
To the rock where the cormorants stand.
Fix the vermilion feather,
Send down the mackerel line –
The lead plumbs far to the coral bar.
Is there fruit on the thorny vine?

We wait in baited silence –
Till Ben's sudden tug on the string!
Hold the rowlock, here's his first pollock   *Fishing*
Fit for a fisher king.
Then, though many a slippery mackerel
Be born to blush unseen,
For Mummy's dish comes a rush of fish,
So she's the pearly queen.

Take care, little ones, on the jetty
Beware the beckoning sea –
One slip, one tip, and you're in for a dip   *"The Slip"*
Or a trip to eternity.
Rufus' the hand that did the deed
Ben the victim who over-
-toppled and …SPLASH, he was gone in a flash.
Thank God for the four-leafed clover!

Ireland's air is a prism
Of every paintbox hue.
Ireland's night is flagged with light   *The village*
(Though her weather be seldom true).
Cinnabar red the houses
The Guinness black as a flue,
Sullivan's cheeks are as tanned as his breeks
His lobsters are midnight blue.

Now I long for Caragillihy
And Dogey's wormy paw –
Where the seagulls wheel and the submarine seal   *A memory*
Displays his whiskered jaw.
I'll go back there one summer
Where the shrimps ride in on the wave;
Where the bumble bee has his blackberry tree
And the furry vole his grave.

***

For the last days of our holiday
Again we put to sea
From the coast of Connemara *We move on*
By old Yeats of Ballylee.
Inishbofin, Inishbofin,
Sing your mysterious song
Where the coneys play and the donkeys bray
And the walks are five miles long.

We came to find the *Doonmore* –
Alas, what should befall –
To us the *Doonmore* very soon more *A flurry on*
Seemed like Do-the-boys Hall. *arrival*
We tramped the lonely evening road.
At last, to loud hurrays
Our luck struck sound, for we had found
Our night turned into *Day's*.

Past Cromwell's ruined fortress
The jellyfish sail in;
In pools, like mines sea-urchin spines *The island*
Lie in wait for tender skin.
But the sands are as soft as sugar,
And cowries thick from the sea;
There are bright green bikes for 3-speed hikes
And *The Lobster Pot* for tea!

The fields are full of haycocks,
In mounds the peaty turf.
The giddy crags they call the Stags
Brew witches' brews of surf
The wagtail goes his pebbled way,
The curlew cries alone,
The boats lie fast, as in polished glass
Ringed with emerald stone.

Legend tells: two sailors
Ashore one wintry night
By Bofin lake their fire did make –   *A local tale*
Out sprang a water sprite
And after her a snow-white cow –
They chased, the girl dived back
To her lily land, and in their hands
Not cow's tail, but… seawrack!

So never, they say, on Bofin
Lay hold of a white cow
Or in seven years will disappear
All that you see now.
Treasure well this island   *Envoi*
And the memories of our stay.
And seven years on, it'll still be the one
For an Irish holiday.

WICKAM
    (For Gabriel *and* Ander)

By the low sea wall a lonely
hydrangea beckons, the latch clicks,
past whitened driftwood the A-frame's
duck-egg blue veranda returns
far waves of light to the Solent
from where Nab tower reigns like Neptune
over Bracklesham Bay and seems
to point to this house (your writing –
cabin, potato patch, pirates'
dens and shingled rampart down to
the sea) as the home port for Love

Mustardy lichens crown the roof
with slow confetti, by the bed
poppy, cornflower, and scarlet
pimpernel sow their needlepoint,
below 'Night Fishers' catch moonbeams,
and had *Iggulden's Dangerous
Book for Boys* on the shelf foretold
your wedding, it would have pictured
kite surfers, as they tack, lift, and
take off again into the Sun,
their wake streaming behind.

A VILLANELLE FROM RICHARD HAKLUYT
   (For the Company that bears his name)

It pays to listen, when there's much to tell.
Elizabeth invented my vocation –
I kept my counsel. She rewarded well.

Paris was where I came to learn the thrill
(if one has ears) from useful conversation.
Silent, I listened: they had much to tell.

When fresh horizons cast a different spell,
to chart the English and their *'navigations'*
became my life's work. Fame rewarded well.

And now my name lives on (if you don't sell)
in *this* bright corporate reincarnation –
for all my insight, I could not foretell

how soon my offspring, from an acorn-shell,
would put on limbs that reach to every nation.
How is the winning DNA encoded? Well,

quite simple really: two things have to jell –
hard work and buccaneering inspiration.
While both continue, you've still much to tell.
For this, your Founding Spirit's toast: Fare well!

SELF PORTRAIT OF THE NPG

Praise? Yes, for those who've gone before:
Stanhope, Macaulay, Carlyle, Alexander,
the corner-stones. But they'd not have us squander
words on them, knowing there's always more
ahead to get on with. Could it be incorrect
to use our 150th celebration
as a moment to rediscover the British nation
through the Gallery's eyes? No. Then enjoy
how portraits on these walls help us reflect
on what we were, and are, and can become:
fun, fashion, and variousness for some;
for others, the values time does not destroy –
and here is where our children have to start.
Five generations is not long for art.

A POEM FOR KEW
Wordsworth's ghost

Westminster Bridge? Here's something far more fair
old Earth can show: O City passers-by,
I praise the semi-quincentenary
the *Royal Botanic Gardens* mark this year,
which like green lungs return their purer air
to London's heart and its unquiet sky;
while Wakehurst, as I hear, sends words to fly
like migrant swifts: 'Save all seeds everywhere'.

I never dreamed in my immortal sleep
of treetop walks; or crocus, daffodil,
holly and witch-hazel crowding dells so deep
they bring to life again my poet's skill.
Dear Friend, these gardens may you treasure and keep,
till Thames no longer glides at his sweet will.

[Won the Kew 250th Anniversary poem competition, judged by Roger McGough.]

OLYMPIC MESSAGE

An un-named hoplite ran for his city's glory
a new moon rose through silvery olive trees.
Athens memorialised the battle story,
minted the moon on her silver currency.

From the Marines' *Iwo Jima* monument
we once ran through Washington DC,
Fall's leafy gold lit our progress, spent
like ticker-tape at a civic jubilee.

Some did it to express the common weal,
some to raise funds for a deserving cause;
others fulfilled a personal ideal
or chased the dragon of their peers' applause.

True marathoners only run for love,
to feel their freedom in each fleeting mile
for whom time clocked, if it can improve
on last time, is the only prize worthwhile.

***

For 'love' and 'freedom' – yes, and such words bleed
to remember those who ran from start to finish
up Normandy's beaches in our hour of need,
whom today's lies and shame cannot diminish.

And from the Greeks two thousand years ago
the flame now signals and the race relays
a sterner lesson we still have to know,
if we would hold the pass for peaceful days;

that cost at which our leisure hours were won,
the will to face life's older Marathon.

BALLOON OVER LONDON

Ascent
of the Nassau Balloon.

On Monday evening Mr Green made a
very beautiful ascent in his monster Nassau Balloon,
from the grounds of Cremorne House, Chelsea, which were
crowded with company to witness the spectacle. There was some
novelty to attract the spectators and to amuse them. Amongst the 'intrepid aeronauts' was Mr Thomas Matthews, the Clown of Drury Lane Theatre, who regaled his companions in the car, and the thousands of persons who surrounded it, with the favourite ballad of "Hot Codlins". Mr Matthews was equipped in full theatrical costume; the rest of the party in clothes more appropriate for an aerial trip. The ascent was a fine one; it took place shortly before 7 o'clock, the wind blowing slightly from the west. The balloon was carried east by north,and passed over Chelsea Hospital, the new Bridewell and the Middlesex end of Westminster Bridge Then directly over the Post Office, going toward Haggerstone, Dalston and Clapton, over Stamford Hill, toward the reservoir of the New River. The abrupt change of temperature which took place in the space of about
four minutes (the altitude having varied from between 1000 or
2000 feet to 6500) produced a sudden shivering in the aeronauts. After being in the air about two hours and twenty
minutes, the balloon was safely landed in a large
marsh, at Tottenham, near the residence of
Mr H.L Small, a director of the Northern
& Eastern Counties Railway. Mr
Small and his family hospitably
received the adventurous
company. When at
a height of about
3000 feet, Mr
T Matthews,
upon being
requested
sang
a
new comic song
called "Pigs'
Pettitoes", which
was rapturously
encored.

An engraving of Mr Green's balloon may be found on page 69 of The Illustrated London News *for 2 August 1845.*

The Found Balloon

I found the article about Mr Green's Balloon in the *Illustrated London News* (ILN) for 2 August 1845 which had belonged to my wife's father who bequeathed it to her with a large number of other ILNs, since bound to protect them.

I decided it would be fun to use the wording of the ILN article to 'reinflate' the balloon in its original shape, by using the exact words of the article still in their right order.

I allowed English Professor Ricks (who was teaching in Boston at the time) to have 'my' rebuilt balloon published in the current issue of the UK/US magazine *Literary Imagination* Vol 15 Numb 2 2013.

LOWER WEST SIDE 1962
   (For John Lucas)

Leave the Hip Bagel at Bleecker
and Macdougal round 1 a.m.
Look for a Subway, heading for Birdland.
What have we here? Two patrolmen

at this moment wholly engrossed
beating a handcuffed guy to the ground
to stuff his bloody & no doubt awkward
shape into the rear of their Chevy.

Before crossing, on a bagel wrapper
jot their number – feel better already.
Fifteen minutes on, still chewing
it over, searching for the Uptown 9

to 52nd, when a blue and white
police-car pulls out from the corner.
Wave them to a halt, with the received
pronunciation of the innocent

report it through the rolled-down window
("Where I come from, this sort of thing
would not happen. Do you want
a name and address, perhaps also

a witness statement?"). After completing
my world citizen's civic duty,
am puzzled at first by their laconic
non-reaction. A full ten

seconds elapse, before it dawns
with a rush of blood: the same car's
back on the beat, rear seat empty.
Lullaby time, I decide....

ENOUGH AND PLENTY

Here's the gouache that Keith Vaughan practiced on,
signed '52, I bought it from Agnews.
An American already owned the large oil,
and wanted this too. I just couldn't let him.

The full Vaughan Journals are a good read,
but I haven't included them in the *Selected*.
That's why I had to say something here,
He told us he'd chosen from forty-eight notebooks!

The cancer had been lurking some time. Vaughan said
"Suddenly the decision came that it must be done.
I cannot drag on another few years. It's a bright
sunny morning. Full of life…" *4 November 1977 9.30 am*

The capsules had been taken with some whisky, Vaughan wrote
"65 is long enough for me. It wasn't a complete failure, I did some…"
[The editor states here 'words lapse into illegibility'] They do not,
I saw, at the Hammersmith exhibition, Vaughan's own handwriting,
He had written clearly "I did some good work".

UNCOLLECTED FRAGMENT, 1935
(after the Letters of Wallace Stevens)

Dear Mr Stevens,
             I write to say how much
I admire your erudite correspondence.
While noting, however, your view that *'Man is
an affair of the cities',* I did bridle
a bit over *'Study gives the anchorage
of thought, the place to spring from, and poetry
the adventure'* since you also claim *'Art must
fit in with other things, it must be part of
the system of the world.'*
                 For, if *'Italians
have as much right to take Ethiopia
from the coons* (your own word) *as the coons had to
take it from the boa constrictors',* where does this
leave you? Those snakes never lived in Africa.
Truly,
       Comedian as the letter V.

IN THE LOANING
"Spoken for in autumn, recovered speech having its way again, 1 gave a cry…"
(Seamus Heaney)

Even in old age every word spoken
was meant to carry its weight for
the world he was still ready to live in,
a stitch of time – maybe that final autumn.
Whatever the pitfalls, he'd always recovered
with grace from stumble, error of speech
from the stroke, or the fear of having
missed his last chance to dodge its

calamity. The poem, he knew, was a way
to take a deep breath again
and prepare for anything. It's what I
admire about my 'birthday-cousin', who gave
us all such an example, such a
lesson in humility, it could make one cry.

FIXED POINTS

These are such moments
as poems were made for, pure
singularities,
the flagrant coincidence
that gives you the front seat when

a stoat snatches coot's
egg, an antler sheds, a hawk
picks a willow-tit
from thin air, or a wheatear
landfalls off course at Cape May.

Stark witness clamours
for a psalmist's praise, a seer's
magnification,
to save the miraculous
instant from oblivion.

With music too: when
soprano cadences un-
hinge the ear, tears brim
unstopped at the eye:
                    Oh then
let the poem come quickly!

UP TO DATE

("The Oblate Missionaries were the first non-Native settlement in the Okanagan Valley. They worked at Kelowna from 1859 to 1906.")

Rusting away at
Father Pandosy's Mission
lie old haybalers,
diamond harrows, logging tongs,
handploughs, iron pots, grindstones;

there are slipscrapers,
potato hillers, wheel hoops,
bucksaws (with prairie
fiddles to keep them tight),
cow bells, ice tongs, branding irons,

ensilage cutters,
wrenches, tobacco planters,
crowding each other
under barn roofs, abandoned
to the tooth of wind and dust;

in the grass there's more
skeletal machinery,
the grain cleaner was
by A.T. Farrell & Co
of Saginaw Michigan;

the tractor came from
H.P. Saunderson & Co
of Bedford England:
with the 'Danny Boy' cement
drum, all once state of the art.

Energised relics,
does their half-life still transmit
some faint signal for
microwave receivers and
fibre optic antennae?

Perhaps the lesson
of the 22-year old
who left France for Faith
is: know-how may come and go,
courage is not invented.

[Special Commendation 22nd *Poetry Life* Open Competition March 2003]

TEENAGE LINES

It is a terrifying fantasy to live;
Torn by the momentary truth, to reel
and stagger, drunk with the stupor of stale thought.
What reads aright one instant is the next
by the reflection of the mirror petrified
into insanity. Nor can I understand
which world we live in. Reason, an adulterer,
begets base imitations of the Truth,
being itself untrue. What use the minor balance
in the chaotic madness of the whole?
To dream a nightmare is to point the real
To live one is to doubt reality.

Sherborne
27.6.55

CATCHING UP

I read late Ashbery mainly for the titles,
meaning by this not to be dismissive
of a poet's greatness, only to assert
the reader as his necessary counterpart,
without whom it's only the sound of one hand clapping.

Last time in New York I bought 700 pages
of his work, determined to immerse myself
in serious exploration, still feeling that earlier thrill
as his hand first reached from the mirror. Why is it now
I seem to get more from someone's PhD thesis
about him (which I've already read twice)
than I do from most of his poems the book refers to?

It's not that I shy off making an effort: Aeschylus,
the Pindaric ode, the Chinese misty poets –
get your head down, burn the candle, it always turns out
to have been worth it. And I like the idea of what slips
between the interstices, the background, the divine quotidian,
the flickering nano-seconds of the present moment.

So I look down the list of contents of Notes from the Air.

RETROSPECTIVE

Why does life go on
imitating art? Take that
painting by Michael
Andrews, 'A man who sudden-
ly fell over'. The poet

laureate workshopped
at my school once, and propped up
a postcard of it
for the boys to write about.
Playing the woman's part, mine

was in tanka form:
'There, my husband has / fallen.
Should I feel guilty /
or simply glad oft release?...'
In Wilton's Restaurant last night,

at a table with
six guests, the man at one end
just crashed to the floor
sideways in his chair, and lay
there as if being painted.

None of the others
moved, supposing perhaps they
were in the picture,
or angling to remember
what he reminded them of.

The waiters skirted
round, till at length someone thought
to restore him to
the upright. What will come next?
Not 'The Four Horsemen' I hope.

SONNET FOR JOHN BURNSIDE
   (died 25 May 2024)

I met him in Norwich for a poetry session.
Later, on my piece for *Poetry in the Blood,*
he'd let me phone to ask a personal question
and then discuss it, if both were in the mood.

As for what he called 'divine quotidian',
it meant here & now, beauty of the unremarked.
Professor Bate writing warmly for *The Guardian*
had Burnside and Wallace Stevens together marked.

In *History* he sounded his late alarm
"how to be alive in all this gazed upon
and cherished world, and do no harm."
He'll never know, but what about his son?

Let us hope that youngster, with the same kite
"all nerve and line", can reach as high, and write!